## BIG PICTURE PRESS

This edition published in the UK in 2021 by Big Picture Press
First published in the UK in 2019 by Big Picture Press,
an imprint of Bonnier Books UK,
The Plaza, 535 King's Road, London, SW10 0SZ
Owned by Bonnier Books
Sveavägen 56, Stockholm, Sweden
www.templarco.co.uk/big-picture-press
www.bonnierbooks.co.uk

ISBN 978-1-78741-821-9

Printed in China

FSC
MIX
Paper from
responsible sources
www.fsc.org
FSC® C104723

This book was typeset in
Core Circus Rough and Neutraface Text
The illustrations were created digitally

Edited by Susie Rae, Phoebe Jascourt
and Katie Haworth
Designed by Nathalie Eyraud
Production by Emma Kidd
Consultant: Camilla de la Bedoyere

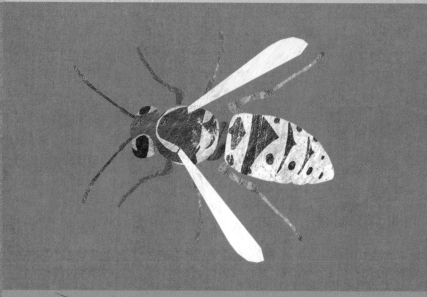

# THERE ARE
# BUGS

## EVERYWHERE

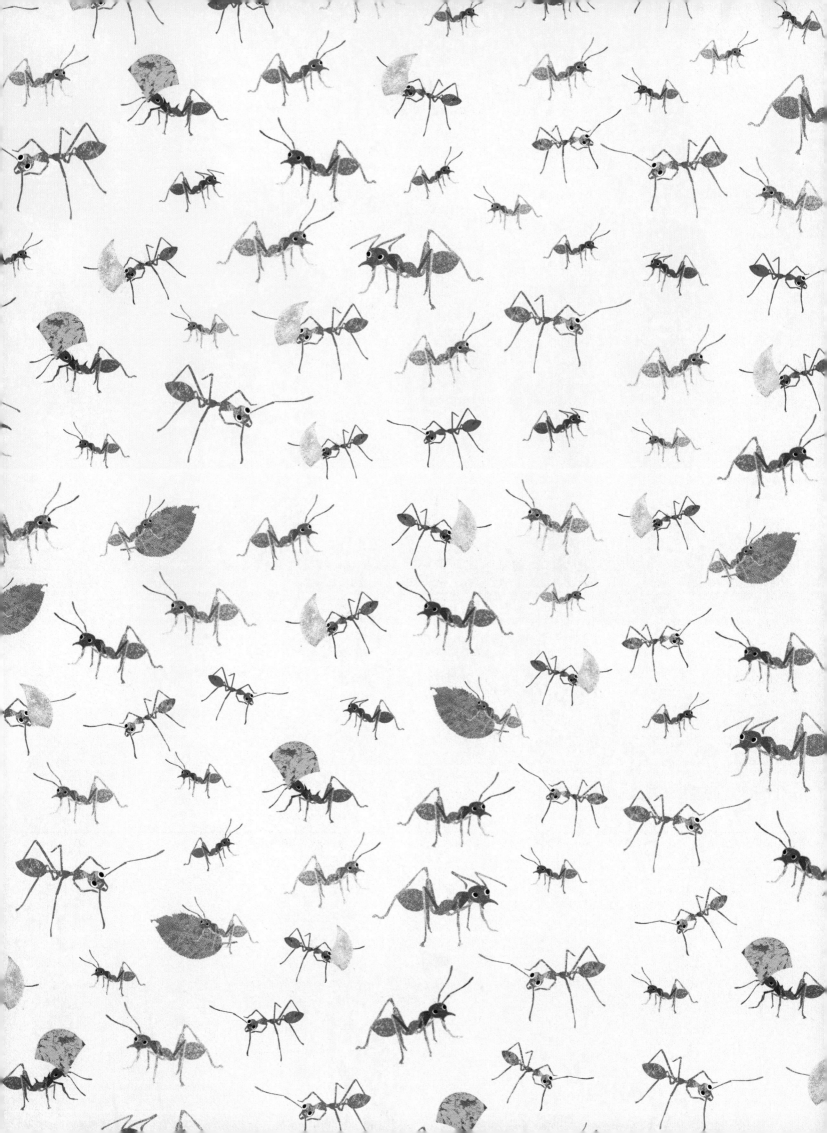

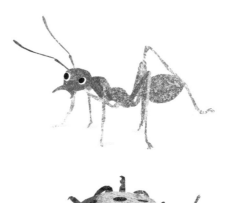

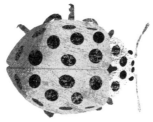

# THERE ARE
# BUGS
## EVERYWHERE

## ILLUSTRATED BY BRITTA TECKENTRUP
## WRITTEN BY LILY MURRAY

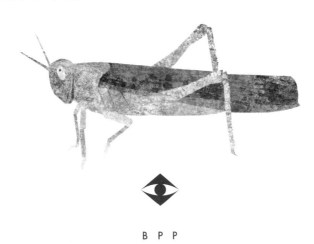

BPP

# THERE ARE BUGS EVERYWHERE

The world is alive with bugs. There are millions of different species. In fact, there are so many that no one knows the exact number. You can find bugs almost anywhere – scurrying underground, fluttering through the air or gliding through water. Hundreds live in your house and some even live on your skin!

Spider

Horsefly

22-spot ladybird

7-spot ladybird

Dragonfly

Chan's megastick

Cicada

Mosquito

Stink bug

Orchid mantis

Centipede

Horned dung beetle

Striped shield bug

Scorpion

Peacock butterfly

Madagascan sunset moth

Wasp

Winged termite

Hewitson's sabre wing butterfly

Swallowtail butterfly

Honey bee

Mayfly

Japanese boxer mantis

Cockroach

Grasshopper

Stinging rose caterpillar

Giant leaf katydid

Leafcutter ant

Titan longhorn beetle

Some of these bugs are record-breakers! Which bug do you think is the strongest? Now see if you can spot the longest, the noisiest and the fastest flyer.

# IT'S A BUG!
# (SO WHAT *IS* THAT?)

The creatures that we call 'bugs' belong to a group known as arthropods. All arthropods have six or more legs, and their bodies are divided into parts (or segments). They also have an exoskeleton (a hard outer covering).

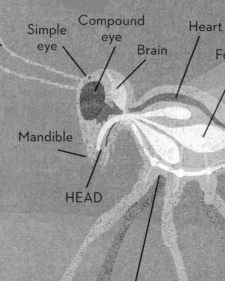
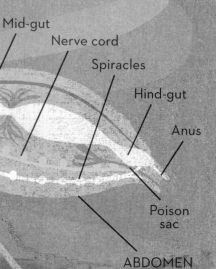

Wings

Antennae

Simple eye

Compound eye

Brain

Heart

Fore-gut

Mid-gut

Nerve cord

Spiracles

Hind-gut

Anus

Mandible

HEAD

THORAX

Poison sac

ABDOMEN

## INSECTS AND TRUE BUGS

There are more species of insect than any other animal group, with around 930,000 discovered so far. All insects have six legs, and bodies made up of three parts: the head, the thorax (the middle section) and the abdomen (just behind the thorax).

## HOW BUGS SEE

Most bugs have large eyes, known as **compound eyes**, made up of lots of different light sensors. These help bugs to detect movement, but they make it harder to spot smaller details. Many arthropods can also have **ocelli** or simple eyes, which detect changes in light.

## TRUE BUGS

**True bugs** are a group of insects that includes shield bugs, assassin bugs and bed bugs. All true bugs have a beak which they use to pierce and suck on their food.

Striped shield bug

# RECORD-BREAKERS
Did you guess which bugs on the last page were record-breakers?

The **horned dung beetle** is the world's strongest bug. It can pull up to 1,141 times its own weight – that's the same as a person lifting six double-decker buses!

The **horsefly** is the fastest flying bug, reaching speeds of up to 145km/h (90m/h).

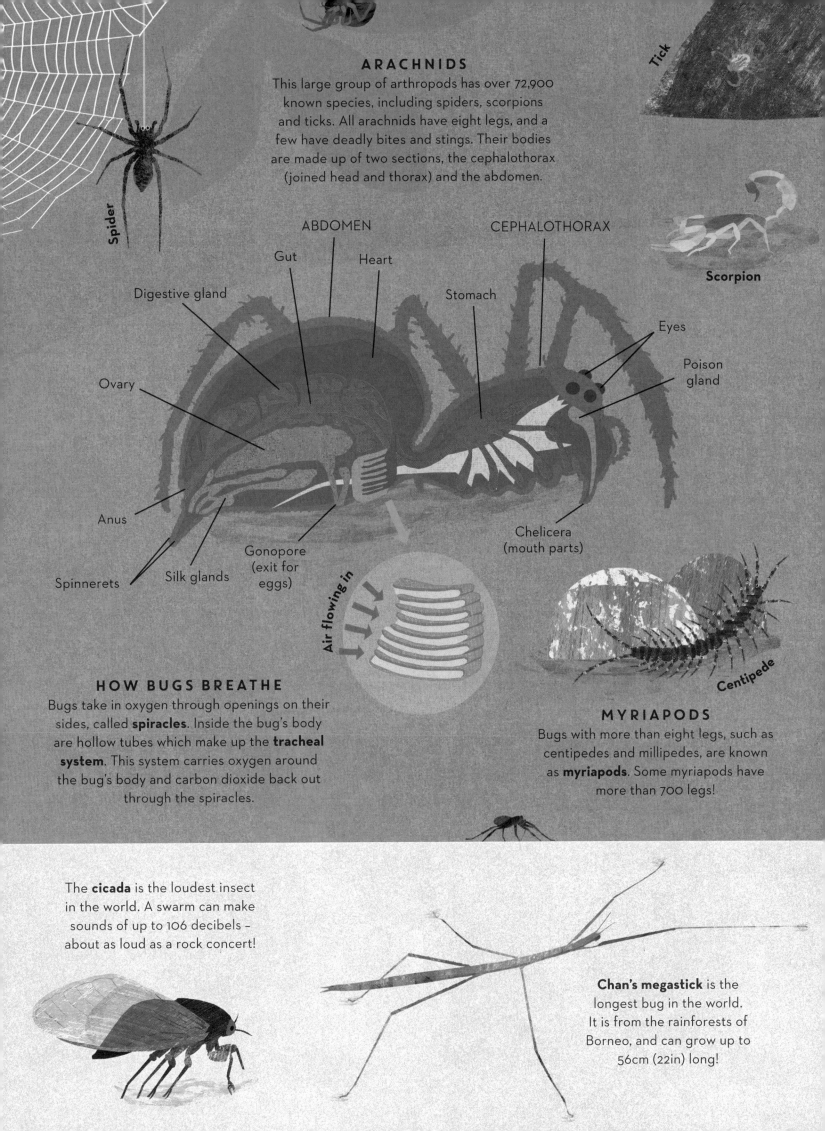

# ARACHNIDS

This large group of arthropods has over 72,900 known species, including spiders, scorpions and ticks. All arachnids have eight legs, and a few have deadly bites and stings. Their bodies are made up of two sections, the cephalothorax (joined head and thorax) and the abdomen.

Tick

Spider

Scorpion

ABDOMEN

Gut

Heart

CEPHALOTHORAX

Digestive gland

Stomach

Eyes

Poison gland

Ovary

Anus

Spinnerets

Silk glands

Gonopore (exit for eggs)

Chelicera (mouth parts)

Air flowing in

## HOW BUGS BREATHE

Bugs take in oxygen through openings on their sides, called **spiracles**. Inside the bug's body are hollow tubes which make up the **tracheal system**. This system carries oxygen around the bug's body and carbon dioxide back out through the spiracles.

Centipede

## MYRIAPODS

Bugs with more than eight legs, such as centipedes and millipedes, are known as **myriapods**. Some myriapods have more than 700 legs!

The **cicada** is the loudest insect in the world. A swarm can make sounds of up to 106 decibels – about as loud as a rock concert!

**Chan's megastick** is the longest bug in the world. It is from the rainforests of Borneo, and can grow up to 56cm (22in) long!

# BUGS HAVE BEEN AROUND FOR AGES

Bugs have been around for a really long time. There have been arthropods in the oceans for over 500 million years. Then, around 480 million years ago, insects' ancestors were among the first animals on land. There was even a time, known as the Carboniferous period (359-299 million years ago), when giant bugs roamed the Earth.

Isotelus

500 million years ago

**Trilobites** are among the earliest known arthropods. Most were tiny, but some, such as *Isotelus*, grew up to 70cm (28in) long.

Meganeura

Mesothelid spider

**Mesothelid spiders** are living fossils in today's world. Their ancestors first appeared around 400 million years ago.

*Meganeura* was a griffinfly. It lived around 300 million years ago and grew to the size of a seagull.

Silverfish

Oxygen levels 300 million years ago were very high, allowing bugs to grow to enormous sizes. At 2.3m (7.5ft) long, *Arthropleura* was one of the biggest bugs that ever existed.

**Silverfish** are very ancient insects. Those that lived 200 million years ago were very similar to the ones alive today.

Arthropleura

The first insects most likely evolved from a group of venomous crustaceans called **remipedes**. Remipedes are still alive today. They are completely blind and live in underwater caves.

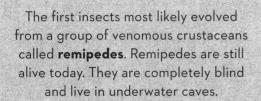

*Remipede*

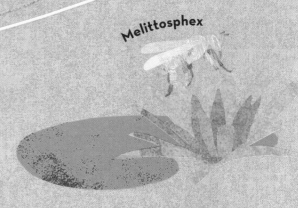

*Hibbertopterus*

Scorpions first crawled out of the water around 430 million years ago. Early scorpions, such as *Hibbertopterus*, spent most of their lives at sea, but also had feet to scuttle around on land.

**Mayfly**

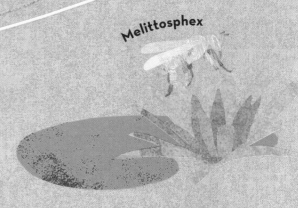

*Melittosphex*

Around 400 million years ago, insects were the first creatures to fly. Plants were growing taller, and flying helped plant-eating insects reach their food source. The first flying insects may have been the ancestors of today's **mayflies**.

The Cretaceous period (around 150 million years ago) brought flowering plants and bugs that fed on them. This included butterflies, ants and the first known species of bee, **Melittosphex**.

**Cockroach**

**Giant flea**

**Flea**

Today

**Cockroaches**, as we know them today, first appeared around 180 million years ago.

During the Jurassic period, giant flea-like creatures lived closely alongside dinosaurs. They were ten times the size of fleas today.

150 million years ago, insects became smaller. This may be because birds took to the skies, and smaller insects could make a quicker escape.

# WHERE DO BUGS LIVE?

Dragonfly

Dragonfly

There are very few places bugs don't live! You can find them in rainforests, deserts, woodlands, wetlands, caves, grasslands, in the freezing Antarctic and in your own back garden. Bugs, in fact, live in more habitats than any other animal group on Earth.

## WATER BUGS

Many bugs live in ponds, lakes, streams and rivers, and you can even find insects in the tiniest pools of water – or above them! **Dragonflies** zoom over water, catching insects in the air.

Water spider

**Water spiders** spend most of their lives underwater but still need air to breathe. They come to the surface to collect large air bubbles which they live in during the day. They leave their bubbles to hunt at night.

Great diving beetle

**Great diving beetles** live underwater where they hunt for bugs, tadpoles and even fish. To breathe, they trap air bubbles under their wings.

Great pond snail

**The great pond snail** glides over underwater surfaces on its slimy, muscular foot. Its tongue is studded with tiny teeth, which it uses to feed on algae and plant and animal matter.

## DESERT BUGS

Most animals struggle to survive in deserts because of the lack of water. Many species of bugs, however, have developed amazing adaptations to live in these hostile environments.

## ALPINE BUGS

In the mountains, temperatures can be extremely cold. Many bugs that live there are dark-coloured to help them absorb the sun's heat.

The dark grey grasshopper **Sigaus villosus** lives in mountains in New Zealand. It uses its long back legs like ski poles, to move across the snow.

The **darkling beetle** survives in the harshest of deserts. It runs to the top of the sand dunes on cool mornings, where it stands on its head to collect water from fog which rolls down to its mouth!

## POLAR BUGS

As there are no land mammals in Antarctica, bugs are the largest animals on land – making **springtails** and **mites** Antarctica's most fearsome land predators!

The **rhagidia mite** is about 1mm (0.04in) wide, and feeds on microscopic creatures. Its body produces a substance called glycerol, which stops it from freezing.

## UNDERGROUND BUGS

Bugs that live in soil feed on plants and animals (alive or dead) and dung. Many live underground their whole lives, some just hibernate there, while others only live there when they're young.

**Mole crickets** spend most of their lives underground. Like moles, they have huge, spade-like front legs for digging, either to find food, or to make a chamber for their eggs.

# RAINFOREST

Tropical rainforests, such as the Amazon in South America, contain mind-blowing numbers of arthropods. A single square mile can be home to more than 50,000 different species! Each species performs a vital role in the survival of the forest. Without these bugs, rainforests as we know them would not exist.

## EMERGENT LAYER
Huge, umbrella-shaped trees, more than 40m (130ft) high, form the **emergent layer**. Butterflies flit from flower to flower spreading pollen.

## CANOPY LAYER
The **canopy layer** sits 30–45m (100–150ft) above the ground. The many flowers here attract insects such as bees, beetles and wasps.

## UNDERSTORY
Below the canopy lies the **understory**. Thick and dense with plant life, this layer is home to countless insects, including bees and stick insects.

**Hewitson's sabre wing butterfly**

**Hewitson's sabre wing butterflies** move so fast the human eye can't follow them.

**Leafcutter ants** harvest leaves from the canopy and carry them down to their nests.

**Leafcutter ants**

**Blue morpho butterflies** drink juices from rotting fruit, dead animals and fungi, and spread spores (which fungi use to reproduce) around the forest.

**Blue morpho butterfly**

**Leaf beetles**

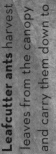

**Orchid bees**

**Orchid bees** travel through the understory, collecting scent from orchids.

## CAN YOU FIND?

Bugs are an important food source for many rainforest animals. How many predators can you find hiding on this page?

The 28cm (11in) wide **goliath bird-eating spider** can easily hunt small birds and frogs. It uses its huge fangs to inject prey with venom.

Goliath bird-eating spider

Most stick insects are masters of disguise. However, the **Peruvian fire stick** is brightly coloured.

**Peruvian fire stick**

**Glow-worm**

**Bullet ant**

**Bullet ants** can be aggressive if their colony is under threat. They have one of the most painful stings of any insect.

**Click beetle larvae** (or glow-worms) make their own light by a process called bioluminescence. This attracts termites for the glow-worms to eat.

**Termites**

The **Titan longhorn beetle** is one of the world's largest beetles, at 17cm (7in) long. Its powerful jaws could snap a pencil in two.

*Titan longhorn beetle*

## FOREST FLOOR

Very little light reaches the forest floor. Spiders and beetles crawl along the ground, which is covered in fallen leaves, rotting twigs and shallow roots.

**Termites** live in huge colonies on the forest floor. They munch up wood and mix it with their poo, creating fungus gardens for them to eat.

Termite mound

# FEEDING

Bugs feast on a whole range of different foods, including plants, other bugs, dead flesh, rotting materials and even dung! It may sound disgusting, but bugs' feeding habits play a very important role in the natural world.

## POO EATERS

**Dung beetles** may eat poo, but they are fussy about the poo they eat. Some will only eat the dung of one species of animal. They feed by sucking up nutritious moisture from the dung.

## FOOD GROWERS

**Leaf-cutter ants** slice leaves with saw-toothed jaws that vibrate 1,000 times a second. The decaying leaves grow into a fungus which feeds the entire colony.

## PLANT MUNCHERS

**Caterpillars** have tough, sharp mandibles, or jaws, which they use to munch through leaves.

## CARNIVOROUS BUGS

**Dragonflies** hunt for midges and mosquitoes. Their compound eyes contain as many as 28,000 lenses, which help them to look in many directions at once.

## NECTAR DRINKERS

The **hummingbird hawk-moth** has a long tongue for slurping nectar from deep, tube-shaped flowers. Its wings beat 80 times a second, so it can hover while feeding.

## SPONGY MOUTHS

**House flies** and **bluebottles** can't bite or chew. Instead, they cover their food in saliva, which turns it into a liquid. They then suck it up using spongy pads on their mouths.

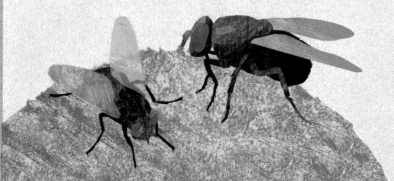

# SWARMS

Sometimes, plant-eating bugs join together in huge numbers, destroying the food crops that people rely on. The most famous swarming bug is the desert locust.

**Locust swarms** have impacted humans for thousands of years. There are stories of these swarms in the Bible and in writings by ancient Egyptians.

When there is an explosion in grasshopper numbers, they come together, forming vast locust swarms of up to a billion individuals.

When they live alone, locusts are known as **grasshoppers**. Their dung fertilises soil and they are a vital source of food for many creatures, including birds, spiders and small mammals.

Each locust can eat its own body weight in plants, and travel up to 130km (80mi) a day. In 1954, a swarm flew all the way from northwest Africa to Great Britain!

# COMMUNAL LIVING

Often, many species of the same bug will live together in large groups, known as colonies. These bugs, which include termites, bees, wasps and ants, live very organised lives, working together to produce food, care for their young and protect each other against predators.

**Honey bees** live in **colonies** containing up to tens of thousands of individuals. Different bees have different jobs to do.

Female bees create wax from their **wax glands**, which they use to build the nest. The nest is full of little pockets called **cells**.

The young, or larvae, are raised in cells known as **brood chambers**. When the larvae are fully grown, they spin **cocoons** for themselves.

Females become **worker bees**. The youngest, known as **nurse bees**, feed bee bread (a mixture of pollen and honey) to the larvae.

The **queen bee** gives off chemicals, called **pheromones**, which control the other bees, and ensure she is the only bee in the colony to lay eggs.

**CAN YOU FIND?**
Wasps often blend in with swarms of bees so they can sneak into the hive and raid it. Can you spot two wasps hiding in this hive?

Older worker bees, called **foragers**, visit flowers to collect nectar, which they suck up through their long tongues.

Male bees become **drones**, whose sole purpose is to mate with a queen. They die shortly after mating.

When a bee visits a flower, pollen sticks to hairs on its body. It brushes the pollen into pouches on its back legs, called **pollen baskets**.

Pollen is mainly used to feed to the larvae, while nectar is turned into **honey**, the bees' winter food.

# STAYING ALIVE

Bugs sit towards the bottom of the food chain, so there are lots of animals that want to eat them! This means they have had to develop clever ways of avoiding predators, such as playing dead or mimicking their surroundings. Some bugs are so good at camouflage, they're almost impossible to spot . . .

### CAN YOU FIND?
These bugs are masters of disguise.
Where are they hiding? Look for:
**Orchid mantis** – looks like a flower
**Chan's megastick** – looks like a stick
**Giant leaf katydid** – looks like a leaf

# MASTERS OF SURVIVAL

### SCARY EYES

When startled, the **elephant hawk-moth caterpillar** puffs out its body, making its eyespots look like snake eyes. This fools predators into thinking they are looking at a much scarier creature.

The bright, contrasting eyespots of a **peacock butterfly** can startle birds and give the butterfly more time to escape.

### TOXIC WARNING

The striking red and black colours on a **ladybird** warn predators that it can release a stinky and foul-tasting chemical if attacked.

### LET'S PRETEND

To avoid being eaten, **click beetles** lie on their backs and pretend to be dead. They can quickly escape by flexing a hinge in their body which hurls them up into the air, producing a loud clicking sound.

Ladybird

Ladybird mimic spider

The **ladybird mimic spider** has cunningly evolved a similar colour pattern to ladybirds. This keeps predators away – even though these bugs aren't foul tasting at all!

### POISONOUS BRISTLES

Some caterpillars, such as the **stinging rose caterpillar**, are covered in stinging hairs. These act as a defence against birds and predatory insects.

### STRANGE HATS

When a **gum leaf skeletoniser** caterpillar moults its skin, it keeps the casing that once covered its head. With each moult, the stack of empty head cases grows until it forms a tower, which it uses to fight off predators like stink bugs.

Stink bug

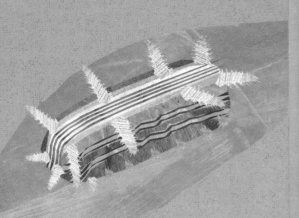

# CLEVER HUNTERS

Spiders are brilliant and efficient hunters. Some hide and then pounce on their prey, while many make intricate silk webs to catch their food.

Like all spiders, **golden orb-weavers** produce silk in their abdomens. To make a web, they squeeze the silk out of little holes, called **spinnerets**, on the undersides of their bodies.

The female golden orb-weaver is larger than the male, and can build huge, wheel-shaped webs, sometimes more than 1m (3.3ft) across!

They prey mainly on insects, but their webs can be strong enough to catch bats and small birds.

Females often spin rotting plants or leaves into their webs to attract prey.

**CAN YOU FIND?**
It looks like some prey has fallen victim to this spider's huge web! Can you find the trapped creatures which the spider can eat for its dinner?

When something lands on the web, the spider plucks the web's silk strings. The vibrations help the spider work out what prey it has caught.

The spider also adds in web decorations, known as **stabilimenta**. These can be zigzags, circles and patterns. No one knows for sure why they do this though!

Golden orb-weavers get their name from the bright colour of their webs.

The golden-orb-weaver paralyses its prey by injecting it with venom from its fangs. It then wraps its meal in a silk cocoon to store it for later.

# AMAZING WEBS

**Funnel web spiders** use their webs as both a trap and a hideout. Silk trip lines at the front of the funnel alert the spider to prey.

**Cobweb spiders** make irregular, sticky webs. When an insect gets stuck in the web, the spider injects it with venom, wraps it in silk and saves it for later.

Some spiders build **woolly webs** out of silk that isn't sticky. To trap their prey, the spiders give the silk an electric charge by brushing it repeatedly with their back legs.

# BUG PARENTS

Bugs will go to all sorts of lengths to attract a mate. Some dance, others bring gifts, and a few even risk their lives. Once their bug babies are born, many parents leave their offspring to fend for themselves. However, some stick around for years, attentively caring for their young.

### EAT MY WINGS

A male **hump-winged grig** rubs his forewings together to attract a mate. He then allows the female to munch on his wings and lap up his haemolymph (blood-like fluid).

### GRUESOME GIFTS

Some species of **male balloon fly** wrap a dead insect inside an oval balloon of silk and then dance around with it. A female flies into the swarm and chooses her partner, who then offers her his gift.

### SMELLY SURPRISE

Female **emperor moths** produce a scent, called a pheromone, to attract mates. Males can pick up the scent with their feathery antennae from up to 8km (5mi) away.

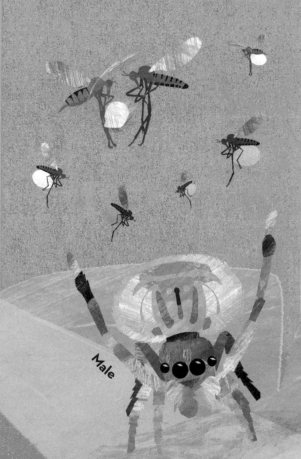

Male

### A RISKY DANCE

Male **peacock jumping spiders** will dance to impress females. They move their legs, vibrate their bodies and unfurl their elaborate fan, revealing its striking shape and colours. This is a very dangerous dance – if the female doesn't want to mate with him, she will eat him instead!

Peacock jumping spiders

Female

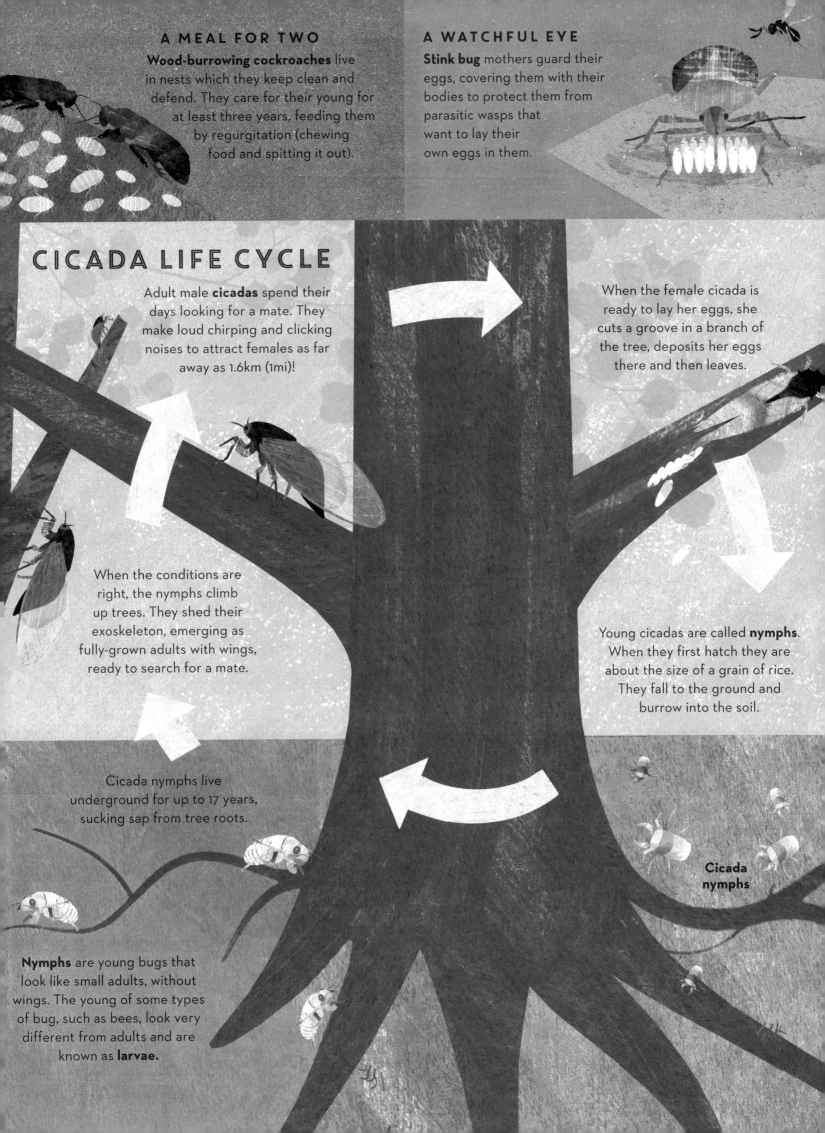

## A MEAL FOR TWO

**Wood-burrowing cockroaches** live in nests which they keep clean and defend. They care for their young for at least three years, feeding them by regurgitation (chewing food and spitting it out).

## A WATCHFUL EYE

**Stink bug** mothers guard their eggs, covering them with their bodies to protect them from parasitic wasps that want to lay their own eggs in them.

# CICADA LIFE CYCLE

Adult male **cicadas** spend their days looking for a mate. They make loud chirping and clicking noises to attract females as far away as 1.6km (1mi)!

When the female cicada is ready to lay her eggs, she cuts a groove in a branch of the tree, deposits her eggs there and then leaves.

When the conditions are right, the nymphs climb up trees. They shed their exoskeleton, emerging as fully-grown adults with wings, ready to search for a mate.

Young cicadas are called **nymphs**. When they first hatch they are about the size of a grain of rice. They fall to the ground and burrow into the soil.

Cicada nymphs live underground for up to 17 years, sucking sap from tree roots.

Cicada nymphs

**Nymphs** are young bugs that look like small adults, without wings. The young of some types of bug, such as bees, look very different from adults and are known as **larvae.**

# MADAGASCAN SUNSET MOTH

The Madagascan sunset moth can only be found in Madagascar, an island off the east coast of southern Africa. With its vibrant, colourful wings, this moth is considered one of the most beautiful in the world. Despite their delicate wings, thousands of these moths migrate huge distances across Madagascar each year in search of plants on which to lay their eggs.

**Eggs**

The eggs hatch into yellow and white caterpillars with black spots and bristle-like hairs.

Omphalea leaves contain **toxins**. These don't harm the caterpillars, but protect them from predators such as ants and birds. The caterpillars can quickly devour entire plants.

**Caterpillars**

**Madagascan sunset moth**

The **Madagascan sunset moths** have just arrived from a long migration, and it's time for the females to lay their eggs. Each moth lays around 80 domed eggs on the undersides of **Omphalea** leaves (the only plant their caterpillars will eat).

## CAN YOU FIND?

Madagascan sunset moths like to drink nectar from all kinds of plants – their favourites have white or yellow flowers. How many moths can you spot slurping up nectar with their long, straw-like tongues?

The Omphalea plants the moths left behind on the other side of the island slowly become less toxic. This means the moths can one day return.

When the moths finally find a new patch of the Omphalea plant, they settle to breed and the cycle begins once again.

They spin a cocoon around themselves, made from silk.

**Cocoon**

At two months old the caterpillars are ready to transform.

After 17–23 days, they emerge as moths.

The moths let their wings dry for up to two hours, then they can fly.

Before their transformation, the caterpillars spent weeks eating Omphalea leaves. To fight back, the plants develop a stronger toxin which can harm the caterpillars.

The moths must now find new plants. They migrate all the way across Madagascar, from the rainforests in the east to the dry forests in the west, flying over mountains and semi-deserts.

The moths have few predators, as their bright colours act as a warning that they are toxic to eat. As the moths fly, their wings appear to change colour, but this is just an illusion.

Madagascan sunset moths fly during the day. By night, they roost together for warmth and protection.

# BUGS AND PEOPLE

Bugs have been vital to humans for millions of years. They fertilise plants, break down waste and are an important food source for animals, including humans. Throughout history, humans have feared bugs but have also been inspired by them. We are only just beginning to realise that bugs are essential to the future of the planet.

### BUG CHARMS

In ancient Egypt, **scarab beetles** were symbols of Khepri the sun god and new life. The scarab was a popular design for jewellery, charms and stamps, and many scarab amulets have been found buried with mummies.

### ANCIENT FOOD

Our hunter-gatherer ancestors relied on bugs for protein. For the ancient Romans, wine-fed **beetle larvae** was a delicacy. Today, many people still eat bugs, and as our population grows, bugs could become a key, environmentally friendly food source.

### TUNEFUL PETS

Since as far back as 1000 BC, the ancient Chinese kept **crickets** as pets, often in elaborate bamboo or metal cages. Crickets were cherished for their singing and fighting abilities. They are still kept as pets today.

## BUG INVENTIONS

Today, research into bugs is at the cutting edge of science. It has led to some fascinating solutions to human problems.

The **bombardier beetle** blasts toxic steam from its abdomen. Scientists studying it have developed a new type of needle-free injection.

**Termite mounds** do not overheat in the sun, due to a system of air pockets which circulate cool air. This has inspired the design of a shopping mall in Zimbabwe which uses a similar system of air pockets to keep cool.

# A WORLD WITHOUT BUGS

Bugs are the invisible power that keeps the world working. But they are under threat, and their numbers are dwindling. So how do we protect them? Here are a few things you can do at home.

Why not make a bug hotel filled with dry leaves, dead wood and hollow tubes? This will make an ideal home for **beetles**, **centipedes**, **spiders** and more.

Plant nectar-rich flowers, such as buddleia and autumn ivy, for **butterflies** and **bees** to feed on.

Dig a pond! This will attract insects such as **dragonflies**, **pond skaters** and **water beetles**.

Scientists predict that millions more species of bugs are yet to be discovered. So get out your magnifying glass and see if you can find the next new species of insect, arachnid or myriapod!

**Spider silk** is stronger than steel and is tough, light and flexible. An artificial version has been created to make medical equipment, machine parts and protective clothing for soldiers.

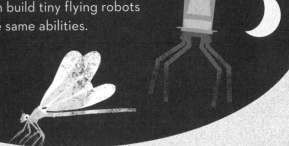

**Dragonflies** can spot moving objects in the dark. Scientists are studying these insects to see if they can build tiny flying robots with the same abilities.

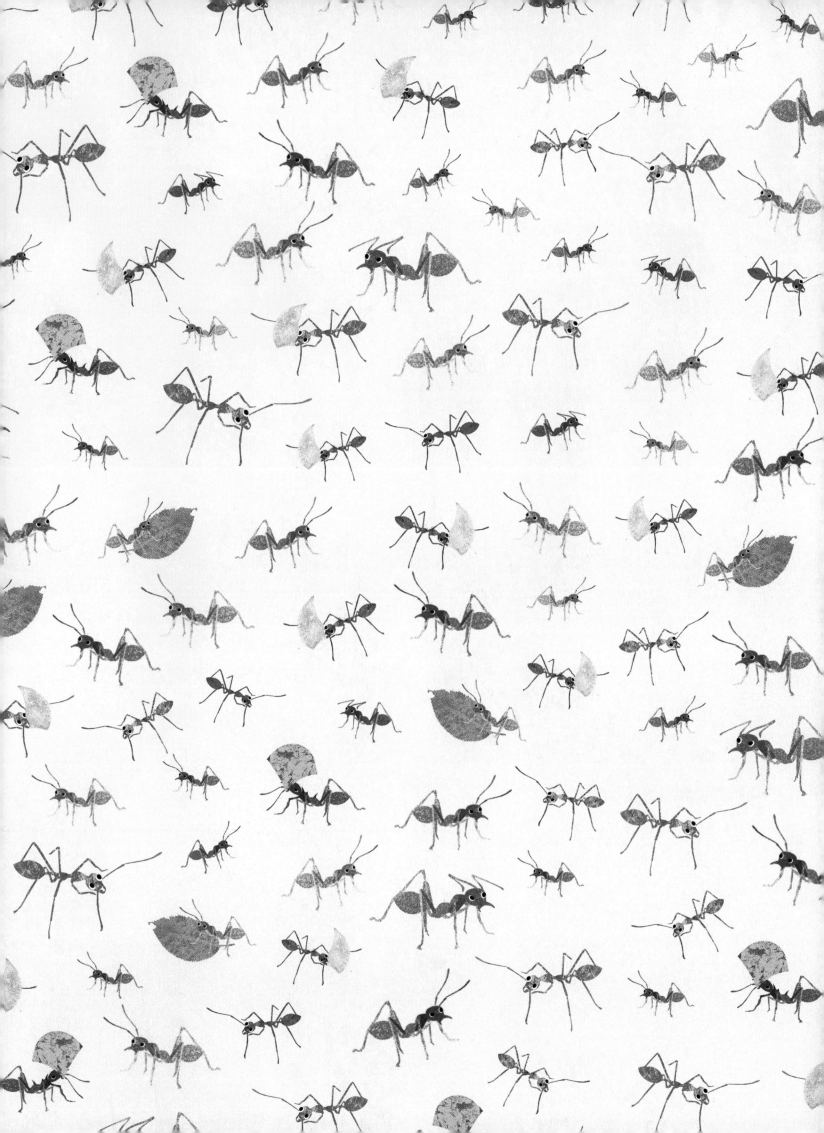

# CAN YOU FIND?

The golden tortoise beetle from North America only grows to around
7mm (0.3in), but it has a powerful survival strategy. When under attack,
it can change colour, from gold to orange to spotted black to brown.
There is a golden tortoise beetle hiding somewhere in this book.
Can you find it?

# ALSO IN THE EVERYWHERE SERIES:

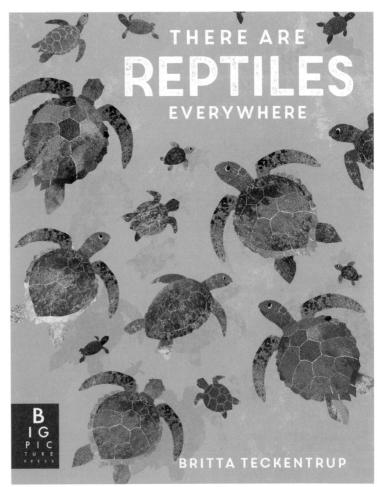

ISBN 978-1-78741-076-3 (Hardback)
ISBN 978-1-78741-775-5 (Paperback)

ISBN 978-1-78741-653-6 (Hardback)